VALLEY of the KINGS

VALLEY of the QUEENS

Text:
Giovanna Magi

BONECHI

THE NUMBERING OF THE TOMBS

It is to John Gardner Wilkinson, one of the founders of egyptology, that we owe the numbering of the tombs in the Valley of the Kings and the chronological cataloging of the pharaohs who are buried there.

In 1927, Wilkinson set out to number the tombs according to a simple but highly efficacious system: armed with a bucket of paint and a brush, he assigned a progressive number to each tomb by painting it on the entrance or on nearby rock. He began numbering with the tomb lowest down in the Valley (that of Ramses VII, No. 1) and proceeded along the main path, numbering as he went on both the left and the right. By the time he reached the top of the Valley he had numbered 15 tombs. He then descended again to count those in the adjacent ravines. The known and numbered tombs are today 62, all bearing the abbreviation KV for King's Valley. But a great deal of the Valley has yet to be excavated.

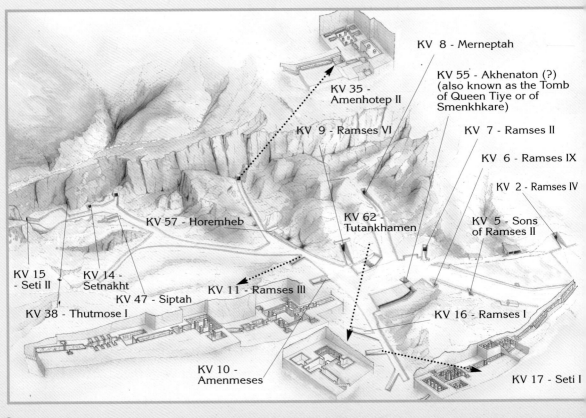

KV 8 - Merneptah

KV 55 - Akhenaton (?)
(also known as the Tomb
of Queen Tiye or of
Smenkhkare)

KV 35 -
Amenhotep II

KV 9 - Ramses VI

KV 7 - Ramses II

KV 6 - Ramses IX

KV 2 - Ramses IV

KV 57 - Horemheb

KV 62 -
Tutankhamen

KV 5 - Sons
of Ramses II

KV 15
- Seti II

KV 14 -
Setnakht

KV 47 - Siptah

KV 11 - Ramses III

KV 38 - Thutmose I

KV 16 - Ramses I

KV 10 -
Amenmeses

KV 17 - Seti I

...l-Qurn: the pyramidal mountain that dominates the Valley of the Kings.

THE VALLEY OF THE KINGS

The valley of Biban el-Muluk, the **Gate of the Kings**: in this celebrated ravine, dominated by a pyramid-shaped mountain often called the "Crown of Thebes," is the necropolis of the great Egyptian sovereigns of the 18th to the 20th Dynasty.

The story of the Valley of the Kings begins with the sudden and unexpected decision of Thutmose I to separate his tomb from his mortuary temple—and moreover to bury his body not in a showy monument but in a secret, inaccessible place. His resolution brusquely interrupted a tradition that had lasted all of 1700 years! His chief architect, Ineni, excavated a shaft tomb in a lonely ravine, cut a steep stairway into the rock, and at its bottom built the sepulcher; this plan was followed by all the later pharaohs.

Ineni himself has provided us with documentation of the utmost secrecy of the undertaking, in a phrase he had carved into the wall of the mortuary chapel: "I alone oversaw the construction of the rupestral tomb of His Majesty. No one saw anything; no one heard." Actually this last phrase is not particularly credible: it is much more likely that the workers may have been prisoners of war who were eliminated when the work was completed.

But the repose of Thutmose I, like that of most of the pharaohs, was of short duration. Systematic plundering of the tombs began early, despite 24-hour surveillance by teams of guards during the entire Pharaonic period. The thieves were of course after the precious tomb furnishings; one of the objects they most coveted was the so-called "heart scarab," the amulet placed on the mummy over the heart to permit the deceased to save himself on the day of judgment, when his actions were weighed.

By a curious twist of fate, these powerful kings were destined not to find peace even after death. During the reigns of the Ramessides, the priests of Amon, once so powerful, lost all their authority. They nevertheless remained devoted to their deceased kings and, in order to ensure them an undisturbed afterlife and to avoid profanation of the tombs, began surreptitiously transporting the royal mummies from one burial site to another. These transferrals were so frequent that Ramses III was buried all of three times! Finally, they decided to prepare a practically inaccessible secret hiding place in the mountain of Deir el-Bahari, where they had a shaft dug to a depth of about twelve meters. A long corridor led off from the bottom of the shaft into a spacious room. At night and in great secret, with only a few torches to provide light, as stealthily as the tomb raiders

3

themselves, the priests took the pharaohs from their sarcophagi in the Valley and laid them all to rest in this cave in the mountain, each with a name shield around the neck for identification.

Some had died recently, some centuries before, some had reigned for short periods and others for decades; some had once been the most powerful rulers on earth. It made no difference. Now they lay all together, in sparse order, one alongside the next. Ahmose, the founder of the 18th Dynasty, lay beside the conqueror Thutmose III; the great Ramses II close by his father Seti I. All in all, the bodies of the pharaohs which were to remain hidden in this anonymous tomb in the heart of the mountain for three thousand years numbered forty.

A young tomb robber named Ahmed Abd el-Rasul, from the village of Qurna, discovered this hiding place by pure chance one day in 1875: for six years he and his brothers succeeded in keeping the secret and became rich from trade in the objects they gradually stole from the royal mummies. Then the secret came out and on 5 July 1881, after lengthy questioning, the young Arab led Emil Brugsch (brother of the famous egyptologist Heinrich and at the time vice director of the Museum of Cairo) to the entrance of the shaft. It is hard to imagine what the scholar must have felt when the flickering light of the torches illuminated the mortal remains of forty sovereigns of the ancient world!

A few days later, the mummies were packed and carried down into the valley, where a ship was waiting to take them to Cairo. What happened then was both strange and moving: on hearing that the pharaohs were leaving their centuries-old tomb, the peasants of the valley and their wives crowded along the banks of the Nile and as the ship slowly passed they rendered homage to their ancient kings, the men firing guns in the air and the women keening laments and scattering dust on their heads and breasts.

Today, the Valley of the Kings is served by a good road that for most of its length follows the route that the funeral procession must have taken.

The tombs are just as fascinating as ever, the countless graffiti on the walls mark the passage of travelers and pilgrims from Greek and Roman through modern times. One of these was the Englishman Dean Stanley, who in 1856 wrote a fine report of his journeys, remarking how seeing the tombs of the Kings was in his opinion tantamount to having seen all of Egyptian religion revealed as it appeared to the powerful of Egypt in the most salient moments of their lives.

The tombs are all more or less alike; that is, with an entrance cut into the rock wall, a sloping corridor about a hundred meters long opening on niches and various rooms the ceilings of which are supported by pillars, and a sarcophagus room at the end.

Top: the English archaeologist Howard Carter.
Bottom: the Italian Giovanni Battista Belzoni.

MUMMIFICATION RITES

*T*he perfect embalming tech-niques used by the ancient Egyptians are believed to be only secondarily responsible for the spectacular state of preservation of the corpses; the principal rea-son would appear to be the ex-tremely dry climate of Egypt and the total absence of bacteria in the air and the sand. Just how was a corpse mummified? The body of the deceased was en-trusted to the hands of special-ists, who began the embalming by using a hook to extract the brain through the nostrils. The skull was then filled with a mix-ture based on liquid bitumen, which hardened as it cooled. The eyes were removed and later re-placed with enameled orbs. Us-ing an extremely sharp stone, an incision was made on the left side of the body and the viscera were extracted. Only the heart was left in place. After being treated with boiling bitumen, the stomach, liver, lungs, and in-testines were wrapped and then sealed in four canopic jars of clay, limestone, alabaster, other stones, or metal, depending on the social standing of the dead man; the heads figured on the stoppers of the single jars—one human, one a jackal, one a hawk, and one a baboon—sym-bolized the four attendant spirits of the dead. The jars were placed in a single container near the mummy. The interior cavities of the corpse were carefully washed with palm wine, dried using a powder of aromatic plants, and finally filled with ground myrrh or with perfumed wood sawdust. Thus prepared, the body was im-mersed in a bath of natron (nat-ural sodium carbonate) for seven-ty days. At the end of this period, during which the fleshy parts dissolved in the natron solution, all that remained was the skin at-tached to the bones. The hair of the men was cut short, while that of the women was left in all its splendid length. At this point, the corpse was wrapped with narrow bindings impregnated with resin on the lower side. Wrapping began with the sepa-rate fingers, then the hand, and finally the arm; then the foot and leg, and so on. Work on the head was more meticulous. A cloth similar to muslin was used in im-mediate contact with the skin. The figure was covered with sev-eral layers of bindings, which ad-hered so perfectly that if they had been removed all together, a plaster cast made from them would have been an exact por-trait of the dead man. The entire body, lying supine, with the hands crossed on the breast or with the arms stretched out along the sides, was then again wrapped in bindings for its entire length. The corpses of the pharaohs merited a precious shroud or a golden case on which were embossed the fea-tures of the dead man.

Above, the rite of mummification painted on a wall in the tomb of Sennedjem. Left: The Four Sons of Horus. During the complex rite of mummification, the viscera of the dead person were sealed into four canopic jars placed in the care of four mortuary deities, the sons of Horus. Their effigies were reproduced on the covers of the jars: the jackal-headed Duamuttef protected the stomach, the baboon-headed Hapi the lungs, the falcon-headed Qebesenuf the intestines, and Imset, with a human countenance, the liver.

The sarcophagus with the mummy of Tutankhamen.

TOMB OF TUTANKHAMEN (KV 62)

Tutankhamen's tomb was discovered on 4 November 1922 by the mission of Lord Carnarvon, directed by the archaeologist Howard Carter. Almost at the base of the tomb of Ramses VI Carter found a stone step, then a second, and so forth until he had uncovered twelve and a sealed door. On the 26th of the same month Carter made a small opening with an iron bar and pushed it through the hole, meeting no obstacles: as his eyes gradually adapted to the darkness, ". . . strange animals, statues and gold—everywhere the flash of gold—emerged slowly from the darkness . . ."

Of all the precious objects in the sovereign's tomb, the most impressive of all was the great sarcophagus: a single, enormous block of quarzite housed in four gilt wooden containers placed one inside the other.

On 12 February 1924, in front of nineteen illustrious guests, a complex winch lifted the ton and a half of granite of the lid. Inside was the first anthropoid sarcophagus (2.25 meters long), in wood, entirely plated in gold and inlaid with glass and semiprecious stones, representing the pharaoh as Osiris.

Inside it lay a second gold-plated, wooden, anthropoid sarcophagus encrusted with cloisonnés of colored glass and semi-precious stones. With the help of eight men, the lid of this second coffin was lifted even if at this stage Carter expected to find a third sarcophagus, he certainly did not expect to find a solid gold coffin weighing 110.4 kilograms! The king wears a false beard and a heavy necklace in gold grains and majolica, and holds the crook and flail sceptres, symbols of the two Egyptian kingdoms. One can imagine with what awe and suppressed emotion Carter approached the contents of this coffin. The mummy was completely covered in gold and jewels. Once again, the delicate, serene features of the nineteen-year old king appeared on the magnificent mask in gold and semiprecious stones that covered the sovereign up to his shoulders. The heavy blue and gold striped nemes with the royal symbols on the forehead, inlaid with turquoise lapislazuli and cornelians, made an impressive sight.

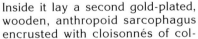

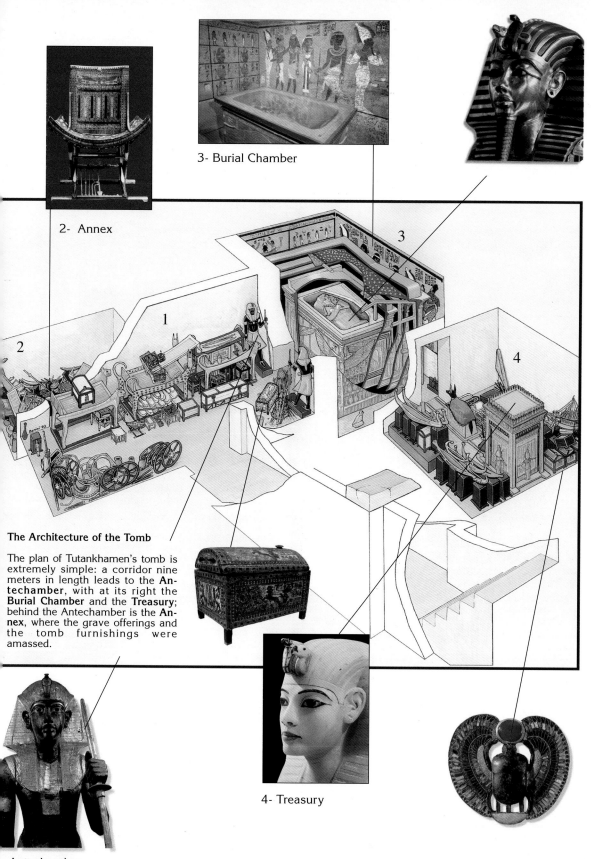

3- Burial Chamber

2- Annex

3

1

2

4

The Architecture of the Tomb

The plan of Tutankhamen's tomb is extremely simple: a corridor nine meters in length leads to the **An- techamber**, with at its right the **Burial Chamber** and the **Treasury**; behind the Antechamber is the **An- nex**, where the grave offerings and the tomb furnishings were amassed.

4- Treasury

- Antechamber

TOMB OF RAMSES VI (KV 9)

Known in ancient times as the tomb of Memnon and as the "La Tombe de la Métempsychose" by the scholars of the Napoleonic expedition of 1798, this tomb was discovered by the Englishman James Burton. Like the other great Ramesside tombs, its entrance is high, about 400 metres above the valley bottom, exactly the opposite of the deeply-dug tombs of the sovereigns of the 18th Dynasty. The front part is the oldest and was begun for Ramses V. The final, enlarged plan is quite linear, with two corridors and two antechambers preceding the sarcophagus room. The latter has an "astronomical" ceiling, entirely decorated with scenes of the sky and frescoes narrating the creation of the sun. The leitmotif is the sky goddess Nut, repeated twice, towering above all and enfolding the western sphere. The many Greek and Coptic graffiti on the walls indicate that the tomb was known and visited from oldest times.

Above: Tomb of Ramses VI, with the goddess Nut and the stellar goddesses. Below: Tomb of Ramses IX, a symbolic scene with the sacred scarab and the sun, Ra

TOMB OF RAMSES IX (KV 6)

This unfortunately quite damaged tomb belongs to one of the last Ramessides of the 20th Dynasty, whose reigns were marked by a long series of domestic disorders and by famines. When it was opened, the tomb was found to contain an enormous pair of skids from the sledge on which the pharaoh's bark was transported.
Another interesting find was several hundred shards on which the tomb laborers had recorded numbers of tools, hours of work, lists of provisions, etc.
The tomb consists of a long staircase leading to a corridor that opens onto two rooms, one of which with four pillars, and a second smaller corridor that ends in the sarcophagus chamber.

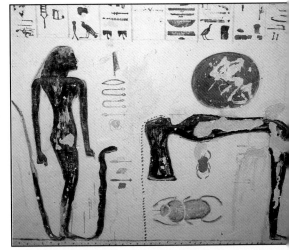

TOMB OF RAMSES III (KV 11)

Ramses III was the second sovereign of the 20th Dynasty and was also the last great pharaoh of the Middle Kingdom, since after his reign Egypt precipitated into a chaotic period of internecine wars and disorders. Ramses III had initiated important administrative and social reforms, and in the eighth year of his reign inflicted a heavy defeat on a coalition of the so-called "Sea Peoples" and Libyan tribes; the great battle on the Delta is illustrated in the reliefs on the walls of the Temple of Medinet Habu, where Peleset prisoners, who later settled in Palestine and called themselves Philistines, are shown along with the other Sea Peoples. In the 29th year of his reign, Ramses II fell victim to a palace conspiracy, as we learn from a scroll known as the Judicial Papyrus, now in the Egyptian Museum of Turin, that documents the capture and judging of the guilty parties.

The tomb is also known as "Bruce's Tomb," after its discoverer, and as the "Harper's Tomb," from the frescoes which show several men playing the harp in honor of the gods—a quite unusual subject in Egyptian art. The pharaoh's sarcophagus, a splendid block of pink granite, was removed by the Paduan archaeologist Giovanni Battista Belzoni and later

A representation of a Syrian.

The corridor leading to the chamber containing the sarcophagus.

sold to the king of France, who exhibited it in the Louvre. The tomb, 125 meters long but dropping only ten meters below valley level, was built on the site of the earlier tomb of the father of Ramses III, Sethnakht, some of whose cartouches can still be seen in the first corridor.

TOMB OF RAMSES IV (KV 2)

The first tomb along the approach to the center of the Valley is small (66 meters long), but contains the sarcophagus of Ramses IV, sovereign of the 20th Dynasty and son of Ramses III. The plan of the tomb appears on a papyrus in the Egyptian Museum of Turin. As early as the 5th century, it was used as a church by a small Christian community in the Valley. The splendid decorations of the tomb are predominately texts, with scenes from the *Book* of the *Dead* (*Am-Tuat*), the *Book of the Gates,* and the *Book* of the *Caverns.*

TOMB OF HOREMHEB (KV 57)

Horemheb, the last pharaoh of the 18th Dynasty, was not of royal blood; from a family of governors, he had been chief of the archers under Amenhotep IV, of whom he was a great friend, and rose to the rank of general; he succeeded Tutankhamen and Ay on the throne, destroyed all symbols of the heretic Atonian religion and surcharged his immediate predecessors' cartouches with his own. Among his most brilliant undertakings was the peace stipulated with the Hittite king Mursilis II. The English archaeologist Edward Ayrton found the name of the general-pharaoh, in hieratic script, on a tablet regarding inspections of the royal tombs in the Valley, and thus succeeded in locating the tomb, which represents a transition from the simple, bent-axis tombs of the 18th Dynasty to the more elaborate ones that were to come; the corridor, after a slight initial deviation, proceeds in a practically straight line to the burial chamber. The eyes of the archaeologists who discovered the tomb were greeted by **bas-reliefs**, which while depicting the usual funeral repertory were brilliantly colored and as perfect, fresh, and light-filled as if they had just been painted.

Above: the great quartzite sarcophagus of Amenhotep II in the burial chamber.
Below: Ramses I offering two vases to the god Nefertum.

TOMB OF AMENHOTEP II (KV 35)

This tomb, discovered by Victor Loret in 1898, is one of the most interesting in the Valley in terms of both architecture and decoration.

The burial chamber contains the great **quartzite sarcophagus**, which when it was discovered still contained the pharaoh's mummy, with a garland of mimosa flowers encircling the neck. In an annex off the burial chamber, Loret found nine more sarcophagi, containing the mummies of the pharaohs Amenhotep III, Thutmose IV, Merneptah, Seti II, Setnakht, Ramses IV, Ramses V, and Ramses VI.

TOMB OF RAMSES I (KV 16)

The founder of the 19th Dynasty was a regular army officer, a general, and the vizier of Horemheb. His reign was very brief, barely two years, but in this period—as witnessed by the bas-reliefs in the hypostyle hall of Karnak—he advanced into Hittite territory "as far as the land of Kadesh." He immediately took his son Seti I as co-regent and chose Tanis as capital of the empire. The structure of his tomb, discovered by Belzoni, is rather spare, since evidently the elderly pharaoh died suddenly while work was still in progress.

TOMB OF SETI I (KV 17)

The tomb of Seti I is one of the most spectacular in the Valley of the Kings, and the pharaoh who was buried there was also one of the most important of his dynasty, the 19th. Son of Ramses I, he was chief of archers and vizier while his father lived. As pharaoh, Seti I continued the policy of eastward expansion: he advanced into Syria as far as Tyre, drove back the Hittite chief Muwatallis, and recaptured Phoenicia. The tomb, discovered in October of 1817 by Belzoni and known at length by the archaeologist's name alone, is 105 meters long. Steep steps descend immediately to a much lower level, where a corridor and a second flight of steps lead to a second corridor ending in a room in which Belzoni found a shaft, evidently dug to confuse unwanted visitors. Belzoni noted a 65-centimeter crack on the opposite wall; after daringly crossing the shaft, he widened the opening and discovered rooms the original builders had hoped to keep hidden. Even so, none of these contained the sarcophagus; as it turned out, Belzoni was only halfway there. More

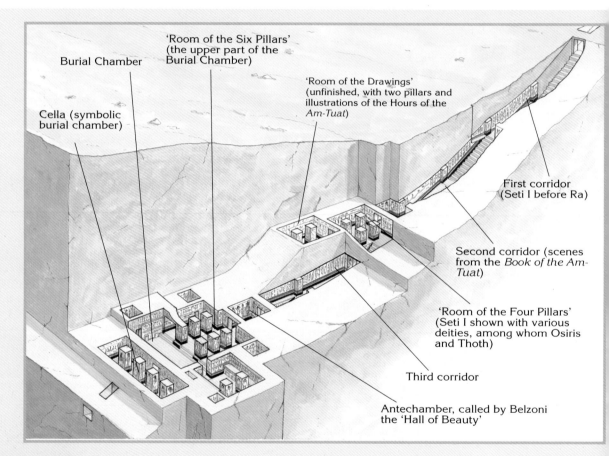

Burial Chamber

'Room of the Six Pillars' (the upper part of the Burial Chamber)

Cella (symbolic burial chamber)

'Room of the Drawings' (unfinished, with two pillars and illustrations of the Hours of the Am-Tuat)

First corridor (Seti I before Ra)

Second corridor (scenes from the *Book of the Am-Tuat*)

'Room of the Four Pillars' (Seti I shown with various deities, among whom Osiris and Thoth)

Third corridor

Antechamber, called by Belzoni the 'Hall of Beauty'

Cross-section of the tomb and a detail of Osiris.

corridors, more staircases, and more rooms finally led him to the sarcophagus chamber—but not the mummy, which was discovered only seventy years later in Deir el-Bahari. The lovely sarcophagus is today part of the Soane Collection in London. What is so odd and unusual about this tomb is the fact that it apparently was supposed to go even deeper into the heart of the earth. Belzoni began exploring a mysterious gallery that starts under the sarcophagus, but after about ninety meters the lack of air and the friability of the rock forced him to stop. Belzoni thought this was the finest tomb ever discovered in Egypt; the walls, columns, and ceilings are in fact literally covered with paintings and bas-reliefs rich in meaning and symbolism.

TOMB OF THUTMOSE III (KV 34)

This tomb was discovered in 1898 by Victor Loret, who had succeeded Gaston Maspero as Director of the Egyptian government Antiquities Service. The entrance to the tomb was hidden in a crevice about ten meters above the valley bottom: two corridors with two steep flights of stairs led to a ritual well that terminated in a vestibule with two pilasters. Sharply to its left was the burial chamber. Its curious form, that of a cartouche, repeats the ovoid of the massive sarcophagus in red quartzite found at the northwest end of the room. When it was discovered, its cover lay broken on the floor—but the mummy of the pharaoh had been safely recovered seventeen years earlier in the Deir el-Bahari hideaway. The tomb of Thutmose III is unique among the Valley sepulchers. The type of writing used here is cursive hieroglyphic, the colors are soft and rosy, and the decorations are all painted, with no bas-reliefs to be found. Thutmose III, called the "Napoleon of Antiquity," was probably the greatest pharaoh Egypt ever had. The seventeen military campaigns he conducted in Syria were all marked by an outstanding strategic sense and a thorough knowledge of military tactics. The list of Thutmose's conquests, inscribed on the walls of the Temple of Amon at Karnak, includes the names of 350 cities that were overcome by his armies. The eighth campaign, conducted near the end of the thirty-third year of his reign, was to have been the decisive attack into the heart of the Mitanni kingdom. Thutmose III died, one mid-March, when he was about seventy years old. He left behind him a politically stable, rich country, an efficient public administration, and a huge empire stretching from the Euphrates to the fourth cataract of the Nile in Sudan.

A statue of the Pharaoh from Karnak, now in the Egyptian Museum in Cairo, and a detail of the walls of the tomb, decorated with scenes illustrating the Book of the Am-Tuat.

THE VALLEY OF THE QUEENS

The Valley of the Queens, known also as Biban el-Harim, opens up at about one and a half kilometres southwest of the Valley of the Kings. The ancient Egyptians gave it the evocative name of "ta set neferu" meaning "place of the kings' sons." From 1903 to 1906 the Italian archaeological expedition led by Ernesto Schiaparelli discovered several tombs, many of which were seriously damaged: some of them showed traces of fire and others were even in use as stables. They contained the mortal remains of queens and princes from the 18th Dynasty.

Khaemwese offering a large feather to the gods.

TOMB OF KHAEMWESE (QV 44)

The red-crowned serpent representing Nekhbet.

The prince Amon-her-Khopsef and the god Khnum.

TOMB OF AMON-HER-KHOPSEF (QV 55)

Detail of the face of Nefertari.

TOMB OF QUEEN NEFERTARI (QV 66)

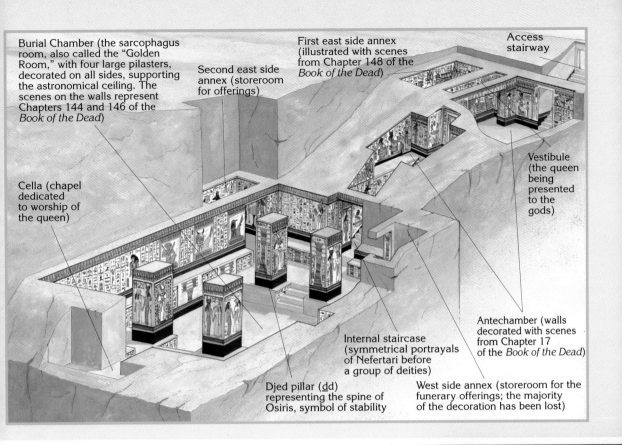

Burial Chamber (the sarcophagus room, also called the "Golden Room," with four large pilasters, decorated on all sides, supporting the astronomical ceiling. The scenes on the walls represent Chapters 144 and 146 of the *Book of the Dead*)

Second east side annex (storeroom for offerings)

First east side annex (illustrated with scenes from Chapter 148 of the *Book of the Dead*)

Access stairway

Cella (chapel dedicated to worship of the queen)

Vestibule (the queen being presented to the gods)

Antechamber (walls decorated with scenes from Chapter 17 of the *Book of the Dead*)

Internal staircase (symmetrical portrayals of Nefertari before a group of deities)

Djed pillar (ḏd) representing the spine of Osiris, symbol of stability

West side annex (storeroom for the funerary offerings; the majority of the decoration has been lost)

Cross-section of the tomb and a detail of one fresco depicting Nefertari.

TOMB OF NEFERTARI (QV 66)

T his tomb, discovered in 1904 by the Italian Ernesto Schiaparelli, was dug into the west flank of the valley for Nefertari, Meri-en-Mut, wife of Ramses II and without doubt the best-loved of the many wives of this great pharaoh, who built the architectural jewel of the Small Temple of Abu Simbel for her. The tomb is 27.5 meters long and lies about eight meters below ground level: since the layer of rock into which it is dug is particularly friable, the walls were bonded with such a thick layer of plaster that their pictorial decoration seems to be in relief. When the tomb was discovered, it was immediately apparent that it had been violated from early times: all the tomb furnishings had disappeared and the mummy of the woman who had been one of the most famous queens of Egypt was nothing but miserable remains. Only the splendid **paintings** remained to bear witness to the fact that this tomb was in its time the most important and loveliest of the entire Valley of the Queens. These depictions have provided us with much information about the complex religious world and the spiritual beliefs of the New Kingdom Egyptians.

The various attempts made between 1934 and 1977 to check the degradation of the tomb obtained no appreciable results; worse, some of the restoration techniques used even altered the colors of the paintings. In 1986, an agreement between the Egyptian An-

Detail of the lintel with the winged goddess Maat, and a pillar with the god Horus.

tiquities Service and the Getty Conservation Institute launched a systematic project for recovery of the tomb. An international team began studying the various problem areas, and it was discovered that rock salt, the major component of which is sodium chloride, was the agent mainly responsible for the damage to the tomb. Restoration work began in 1988. The first step was to apply Japanese paper to immobilize the fragments of detached plaster and prevent them from falling; then and only then was it possible to remove the dust (using dentist's tools), reinforce the plaster, inject a special compound to fill the cracks, and finally smooth over the points of conjunction with fresh plaster.

After cleaning with another special product applied with cotton swabs, the colors regained their original brilliance—so perfect were they that there was found to be no need for any retouching. Work was concluded in April 1992, but for the following three years the tomb was kept under observation by experts, who finally gave their okay for reopening it to the public in November 1995.

TOMB OF AMON-HER-KHOPSEF (QV 55)

This tomb was originally built to contain the remains of another prince and son of Ramses III, and only later became that of Amon-her-Khopsef, son of the same father and Queen Nefertari. Extremely simple in structure—a staircase leads to a square room and a corridor, which in turn leads to the sarcophagus room—the tomb is characterized by decoration in lively, intense colors; an unusual shade of turquoise predominates throughout.

Top: the falcon-headed Horus in the tomb of Amon-her-Khopsef. Bottom: some details of the rich decoration of the tomb of Khaemwese.

TOMB OF KHAEMWESE (QV 44)

Prince Khaemwese, another son of Ramses III and probably the younger brother of Amon-her-Khopsef, was given a tomb that much recalls those of the kings in its ground plan, even though, naturally, it is much smaller. It is, however, the largest of all the tombs of the sons of Ramses III. The decoration is quite lively, with scenes of offerings and tributes in intense, brilliant colors.

TOMB OF QUEEN TITI

Titi was the wife of one of the numerous Ramses' of the 20th Dynasty, perhaps Ramses IV. Her long-abandoned tomb, which has over time been put to many uses—even being made a stable for donkeys!—is in very poor condition despite attempts at preservation; it is nevertheless distinguished by its interesting limestone relief decoration dominated by a light rose color.

The goddess Hathor in bovine form, exiting from a mountain. Giovanni Battista Belzoni left his name inscribed on one of the walls of this tomb.

Detail of the guardians presiding the gates of the Tuat: a crocodile-headed Sobek and a vulture-headed guardian.

TOMB OF PRINCE PA-RE-HER-WENEMEF

Pa-Re-her-Wenemef was another of the sons of Ramses II who died very young and who, like his brothers, was buried in this valley. The decoration of this tomb is quite similar to that of the others of its kind; in other words, the deceased prince is shown being presented to the various gods by his father. The predominant colors here are yellow ocher and pink.

THE VALLEY OF THE ARTISANS

A few kilometers south of Sheikh Abd El-Qurna is the valley now known as Deir el-Medina ("the Monastery of the Town" in Arabic), named after a monastery that stood here during the Coptic period. The "Town" is the ruined Workmen's Village, begun under Thutmose I and inhabited through the five centuries of activity in the valley, from 1550 to 1000 BC, by the craftsmen who built and decorated the royal tombs of Thebes. They were stone cutters, masons, painters, and sculptors, who every morning traveled the steep path over the harsh hills around Deir el-Bahari to the royal necropolis; the children and the women instead stayed at the village, where they cultivated wheat and barley. The workers labored at the royal necropolis eight hours a day for nine consecutive days, and on the tenth—the day of rest—they decorated their own tombs. The teams of artisans (called "Servants of the Place of Truth") were directed by several overseers and were divided into two groups: those who worked on the right walls and those who worked on the left walls. As adepts of the royal tombs, these workers were considered "holders of secrets" and therefore subject to living surrounded by walls. The houses were small and very simple: built one next to the other, in mudbrick, white-washed inside. Generally, they consisted of a tiny entrance, a reception room, a second room, and the kitchen; sometimes, but infrequently, they also had a cellar and a terrace. Nothing remains of whatever decoration they might have had. The necropolis is on the west side of the valley; the tombs are all alike, consisting of a chapel and a small, painted subterranean room.

Aerial view of the Workmen's Village.

THE TOMB OF PASHED

This tomb, from the Rames side era, is located high up in the central sector of the necropolis. A steep staircase leads to the subterranean apartment, in which an unadorned antechamber precedes the burial chamber with its mudbrick walls covered with stucco and painted with tempera. Pashed is shown with his wife Nediem-behedet and his sons, and is referred to as a "Servant of the Place of Truth"; that is, a simple construction worker at the royal necropolis. As an older man, Pashed was perhaps promoted to the post of foreman. Only recently opened to visitors, the tomb is of interest not only for the lively, brilliant colors of its wall decorations, but also for the spiritual and religious significance of the verses of the *Book of the Dead* (*Am-Tuat*) they contain.

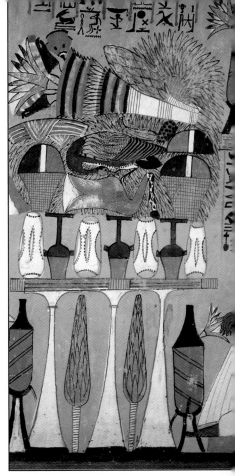

TOMB OF SENNEDJEM

In the vivacity and freshness of its decoration, the tomb of Sennedjem, "Servant of the House of Truth" and an official of the necropolis in the 19th Dynasty, is perhaps the finest tomb in the necropolis. The main burial chamber, which has come down to us practically intact, is all that remains of it; the furnishings that it held are now on exhibit in the Egyptian Museum of Cairo.

Sennedjem and his wife are represented on the back wall of the tomb in adoration of the gods of the otherworld and on another wall at work in the fields.

TOMB OF INHERKA

Under Ramses III and Ramses IV, Inherkha held the office of "Great of the Squad of the Lord of the Two Lands in the House of Truth": a foreman or supervisor, entrusted with coordinating the work of the laborers under him. He had two tombs built, but only the one furthest downstream and closest to the village is decorated in a lively, imaginative fashion.

TOMB OF IPUY

Ipuy, a sculptor under Ramses II, had his tomb decorated with unusual and curious scenes: even if the style is rather sketchy, the wealth of details (for example, the oculist putting drops into the eye of a patient) is such as to make this one of the best known tombs in the necropolis.

Top: the scarab and the necklace of Hathor. Bottom: a scene of fishing.

THE VALLEY OF THE NOBLES

The imposing necropoli of the Middle Kingdom instead lie in the neighboring districts of Assassif, Khokhah, and Sheik-Abd-el-Qurna. Compared with the pharaohs' tombs, these are architecturally extremely simple and all on like plans: an open-air terrace, followed by a vestibule with painted walls illustrating the terrestrial occupations of the owner, and a corridor leading to a niche where a statue of the deceased, sometimes together with those of his wife or relatives, is often found. The paintings in these tombs are characterized by an extraordinary freshness, vivacity, and realism, and provide accurate and valuable evidence of what life at court was like in ancient Egypt.

On the left wall of the corridor in the tomb of Rekhmire, a group of workers sculpt a colossal statue of a pharaoh.

TOMB OF SENEFER

A flight of 43 steps cut into the rock leads into the lovely tomb of Senefer, prince of the Southern City (Thebes) and Superintendent of the Granaries and Livestock of Amon under Amenhotep II.

The anonymous painter of this tomb decorated the ceiling with a marvelous pergola of purple grapes.

In the tomb of Rekhmire, a scene representing the gardeners caring for the fruit trees and a pool with the waters rippled by the wind.

The decoration of the tomb shows Senefer with his wife Seth-Nefer, who was a royal nurse.

TOMB OF REKHMIRE

This tomb, which structurally could be taken as an example of a Theban civilian tomb of the 18th Dynasty, belonged to Rekhmire (or Rakh-Mara), Viceroy and Governor of Thebes and vizier under Thutmose III and Amenhotep II. Both the vestibule and the chapel are decorated; besides being utterly beautiful, the paintings are of immense historical interest since they provide invaluable illustrations, in a great number of scenes, of Egypt's relations with other countries at the time. The liveliest depictions are those in which representatives of foreign countries bring their offerings: the emissaries of the land of Punt (Somalia), carrying ebony, ivory, and ostrich feathers, are clearly identifiable; likewise those of the land of Kefti (perhaps Crete) with their curly hair and long braids on their breasts. Then there are the black Africans of Kush, dressed in panther skins, who bring a jaguar, a giraffe, and monkeys, and the ambassadors of the land of Retenu (Syrians and Assyrians), who lead two horses, a bear, and an elephant.

A group of servants paying homage to their master and the detail of the scene of the barber. From the Old Kingdom onward it was customary for the Egyptians to shave their faces completely and the figure of the barber was a popular one.

TOMB OF USERHET

Userhet, a royal scribe under Amenophis II, had his tomb built and decorated with paintings which are still extraordinarily well preserved today. The unusual scene of a barber shaving his customer in a garden is famous.

TOMB OF RAMOSE

The tomb of Ramose, Governor of Thebes and vizier under Amenhotep III and later Akhenaton, is a splendid example of the delicate moment of transition in Egyptian art toward the new Amarna style.

The tomb was never finished, since during its construction the capital was moved from Thebes to Amarna, but the decoration—mostly bas-relief—nevertheless sufficient to illustrate the refined lifestyle of Ramose and his wife.

One of the most striking works is the scene of the newlyweds at table, dressed in light linen tunics and wearing heavy wigs arranged in ringlets. Like other everyday objects, the wig also evolved through history: from simple and straight in the Old Kingdom, it became more elaborate and voluminous with time.

Above, the bas-relief with Ramose and his wife. Right: on the south side of the hypostyle hall, the famous scene of Ramose's funeral procession, which thanks to its wealth of precise detail regarding the ceremony is considered one of the finest examples of Egyptian funerary art. The servants are carrying furniture: a bed with headrest, four tabernacle-shaped containers holding the possessions of the deceased, a chair with legs in the form of lion's paws, and vases of unguents and scented oils.

A kneeling servant with flowers and a vine-shoot laden with bunches of grapes, and the pressing of the grapes.

TOMB OF NAKHT

This tomb, typical of the 18th Dynasty, is one of the best preserved tombs in the necropolis. The owner was a scribe and astronomer of Amon in the time of Thutmose IV, while his wife was a singer of Amon. In the time of Akhenaton's heresy, the name of Amon was systematically scraped out of all the inscriptions. The aspect of the tomb is that of a classical hypogeum; the accurately-executed decoration is found only in the transverse vestibule.

TOMB OF MENNA

The owner of this tomb was Menna, scribe of the Land Registry under Thutmose IV. To create it, he requisitioned—and enlarged—an earlier tomb. The brilliant paintings that embellish its walls with detailed, lively scenes are generally considered to be among the most elegant compositions in the whole necropolis. The many subjects depicted include the hunt, offerings, and work in the fields.

Offer-bearers on the painted walls of the tomb of Menna.

Two girls dressed in light linen tunics. The first carries a perfume vase and two bunches of flowers

The elegant bas-reliefs in the tomb of Kheruef Sena'a show young women engaged in dance: the typical costume is a short skirt with crossed suspenders tied in the front so as to allow great freedom of movement.

TOMB OF KIKI

A detail of the boat and the baldachin sheltering the mummy of the deceased. An entire wall is given over to scenes of the journey of the dead to Abydos, the sanctuary in which the head of Osiris was preserved.

TOMB OF KHERUEF SENA'A

Kheruef Sena'a was the Intendant of the Great Royal Bride Tiye. This tomb is vast but unfinished. The western part of the court, with its depiction of Amenhotep III's Jubilee celebration (*Heb Sed*), is a true masterpiece.

THE TEMPLES OF MILLIONS OF YEARS

Thus the ancient Egyptians called the funerary temples, popular fixtures above all in the New Kingdom, that were raised to celebrate the cults of living pharaohs. The complex of rites observed during the pharaoh's life secured him eternal life and ensured that he would reign over Upper and Lower Egypt for "millions of years" to come.

RAMESSEUM AND RAMSES II

Ramesseum is the name given during the nineteenth century to the funeral temple built by order of Ramses II on the west bank of the Nile. His "Temple of Millions of Years" was built by the architect Penre on such a grandiose scale—narrates Diodorus Siculus—as to overshadow all the other temples of the time. Unfortunately, today it is only a few ruins: the Osiris pillars on the façade of the hypostyle hall and, like a toppled giant, a mutilated statue of Ramses II seated on the throne: it must have been 17 meters tall and weighes more than 1,000 tons. Diodorus Siculus misinterpreted the Pharaoh's coronation name, User-Maat-Ra, and wrote that the statue was of Ozymandias.

The four Osiris pillars and the head of the colossus of Ramses II.

The monumental complex of Deir el-Bahari and detail of an Osiris pillar in the likeness of Hatshepsut.

DEIR EL-BAHARI AND HATSHEPSUT

One thousand two hundred years after Imhotep, another architect, Senmut, marked Egyptian history with another architectural masterpiece. Queen Hatshepsut, more a patron of the arts than a military leader, ordered a funerary monument for her father Thutmose I and for herself chose an impervious valley consecrated to the goddess Hathor, who in the form of a heifer received the dead in the afterworld. Queen Hatshepsut's monument was in later times abandoned; it became a Christian convent called the Convent of the North, hence the area's present name of Deir el-Bahari; ironically, the Christian use of the structure guaranteed the pharaoh's temple against destruction. The architect/minister Senmut brilliantly exploited the dramatic fan of ocher-colored rock that stretches out behind the monument, which was built according to a new and revolutionary concept in architecture—so new, in fact, that the temple of Hatsheput, called Djeser-djeseru, "more splendid than splendid," by the ancients, is unique in Egyptian architecture. The east-facing temple consisted of a series of vast terraces from which flights of stairs led up to the sanctuary. An avenue of sphinxes and obelisks led to the first terrace, enclosed on the far side by a portico of 22 pillars and flanked by two Osiris pillars. Bas-reliefs on one of the walls narrate the stories of the queen's birth and childhood and of the expedition sent by her to the mysterious land of Punt (perhaps today's Somalia, to judge from the giraffes, monkeys, panther skins, and ivory objects that are shown). On the far wall, 18 niches, large and small, must have held just as many statues of the queen in standing and seated poses. The temple is also home to the 16-faceted pillar so admired for its elegance by Champollion that he called it "proto-Doric." The entire left side of the valley was occupied by the gigantic mortuary temple of Mentuhotep II, who five hundred years before Hatshepsut decided to install hers in the valley had had the same idea. In the main, the tomb reflects the architectural canons typical of the Old Kingdom, but in many respects also heralds New Kingdom tomb structure. The monumental complex consists of a gigantic tomb with a pyramidal tumulus, at the center of which was the king's sepulcher.

The Gatehouse and the Southern Gate, also known as the Migdol Gate, and a representation of Ramses III from his tomb in the Valley of the Kings.

MEDINET HABU AND RAMSES III

For a long time, Medinet Habu was considere nothing more than a rich quarry where larg ready-dressed stones could be found. In Christia times, a village rose and occupied most of the tem ple area—which the Copts called the Mound c Djeme—and in this case, the new utilization resulte in saving many remains that otherwise would hav been lost. The monumental complex of Medine Habu includes the Temple of Ramses III, precede by the shrine of Thutmose I and the chapels of th adoring divinities of Amon. Formidable, almost mil itaristic in appearance, is the fine Southern Gate, al so known as the Royal Pavilion, set between tw towers and crowned by two orders of longitudina windows. Bas-reliefs on the walls further emphasiz the "martial" aspect of this construction: sacrifice of prisoners, the pharaoh leading captured enemie to the god Amon, and so on. The Temple of Ramse III, 80 meters beyond the gate, is one of the mos stylistically perfect buildings in all Egyptian art. pylon 63 meters wide, decorated with scenes of wa leads to a first court with a gallery of Osiris pillar on the east side. Other pylons and other courts lea to the last hypostyle hall, dominated by a statuar group of Ramses III with the god Thoth.

MORTUARY TEMPLE OF SETI I

Seti I begun building this temple consecrated to the god Amon; it was completed by Seti's son Ramses II, who is also responsible for the sumptuous decoration. Although unfortunately the temple has come down to us partially destroyed, the beauty of its reliefs is on a par with Abydos. The vestibule still contains nine of the ten original bundled papyrus columns with closed capitals. In the hypostyle hall there instead remain six, with reliefs of the two pharaohs bearing offerings to Amon. The chapels on the far side of the hall are decorated with reliefs of Seti and his *ka*, Thoth, and Osiris; the sanctuary that housed the sacred bark is likewise beautifully decorated.

The facade of the temple and a bas-relief of the pharaoh on a pillar of his tomb in the Valley.

The Colossi of Memnon as they appear today, and the head of the pharaoh in the Louvre.

THE COLOSSI OF MEMNON AND AMENHOTEP III

The Colossi of Memnon are the remains of the mortuary temple of Amenhotep III and the monumental road that led to it. The two statues, which must have stood to the sides of the entrance to the temple, are 20 meters high; their feet alone are 2 meters long and 1 meter wide.

The sandstone monoliths, represent the pharaoh enthroned with his hands resting on his knees. The southern colossus is in better shape than the other, to which a leg-end is connected. It would appear that in 27 BC terrible earthquake seriously damaged almost all th monuments in Thebes and opened an enormou crack from the top to the middle of the colossu which it also toppled. It was noted that every morr ing, at sunrise, the statue emitted a prolonge sound, likened by some to a sad but harmoniou song. Great historians such as Strabo, Pausania Tacitus, Lucian, and Philostratus corroborated th factand the Greek poets soon turned it into a fin legend. The "singing stone," they said, was Mem non, the mythical son of Aurora and Tithonus an king of Egypt and Ethiopia. Sent by his father to ai Troy, besieged by the Greek army, Memno achieved great glory by killing Antilochus son o Nestor in battle, but in turn he fell by the vengef hand of Achilles. Aurora appealed in tears to Zeus t have her son resuscitated at least once a day. Thu every morning, as Aurora caresses her son with he rays, he answers his inconsolable mother with pr tracted lamentations. Myth aside, the sounds wer caused by vibrations produced in the broken su faces by the brusque passage from the cold of th night to the warmth of the first rays of the sun.